The Rendezvous
Book of **Kerala**
Activities and experiences

www.invismultimedia.com

Concept, Design & Production

Invis Infotech Private Limited
Thiruvananthapuram
Kerala, India - 695 003
info@invismultimedia.com
www.invismultimedia.com

In association with

Kerala Tourism
Park View, Thiruvananthapuram
Kerala, India-695 033
info@keralatourism.org
www.keralatourism.org

Marketing

Culture Vistas Marketing Services Pvt. Ltd.
Thiruvananthapuram
Kerala, India - 695 003
info@culturevistas.com
www.culturevistas.com

First Edition (Economy) June 2006

All rights reserved. No part of this publication may be reproduced, stored in a retrieval system, or transmitted in any form or by any means, electronic, mechanical, photocopying, recording or otherwise, without the prior written permission of the publisher.

This book is sold subject to the condition that it shall not, by way of trade or otherwise, be lent, re-sold, hired out, or otherwise circulated without the publisher's prior consent in any form of binding or cover other than that in which it is published and without a similar condition including this condition being imposed on the subsequent purchaser.

ISBN 81-88698-38-5
Price: Rs. 200/-
(applicable within India only)
Printed and bound by Akshara Offset, Thiruvananthapuram.
© Invis Infotech Private Limited 2006

Publisher's Note

Kerala – the land of pepper, the most popular and indispensable spice in the world. A land, where not only pepper, but other kinds of spices too are grown in abundance. These spice-scented shores have attracted traders from ancient times. We present 101 things that tourists to Kerala must see, do and experience in order to make their journey a memorable and worthwhile one. More than one trip might be required to try out them all but one can choose according to interests, aptitudes and time.

This is an abridged edition of the *Rendezvous Book of Kerala*. We have made every effort to provide accurate and up-to-date information in this publication as far as possible. However, some details such as timings, holidays and activities are liable to change. We request the readers to verify such information prior to their visit. We would be happy to receive your suggestions and feedback. Also please do feel free to contact us for any additional information.

Invis Infotech Pvt. Ltd.

Chief Editor	:	N.R.S. Babu
Editor	:	Dr. Meena T. Pillai
Research & Text	:	S. Jayakumar, Anna Joseph Mathew, M.S. Vidyanandan
Copy Editor	:	R. Vijayaraghavan
Photographs	:	Joshi Manjummel, Nandakumar Moodadi, K. Anil Kumar
Design	:	V.S. Sudheer, K.B. Ajish, M.S. Sreeja, Harikrishnan
Mural	:	Vinod Guruvayoor

Contents

1.	Padmanabha Swamy Temple	05
2.	Padmanabhapuram Palace	05
3.	Kovalam	07
4.	Varkala	07
5.	Kuthiramalika Palace Museum	09
6.	Sree Chithra Art Gallery	09
7.	Valiya Koyikkal Palace	11
8.	Margi	11
9.	Kalarippayattu	13
10.	Palaruvi Water Falls	15
11.	Kuttanad	15
12.	Attukal Pongala	16
13.	Thenmala Eco-tourism	16
14.	Mannarasala Nagaraja Temple	17
15.	Krishnapuram Palace	17
16.	Nehru Trophy Boat Race	19
17.	Niranam Church	19
18.	Champakkulam Kalloorkadu Church	21
19.	Patayani	21
20.	Vastu Vidya Gurukulam & Vijnana Kalavedi, Aranmula	22
21.	Sabarimala	23
22.	St. Thomas Church, Kodungalloor	25
23.	Kumarakom	25
24.	Muniyara, Marayoor	27
25.	Periyar Wildlife Sanctuary	27

Contents

26.	Eravikulam National Park	29
27.	Munnar	29
28.	Hill Palace Museum, Thripunithura	33
29.	Fort Kochi	33
30.	Jew Street	35
31.	Mattancherry Palace	35
32.	Chinese Fishing Nets	37
33.	Malayattoor Church	37
34.	Indo – Portuguese Museum, Kochi	38
35.	Chennamangalam Synagogue	38
36.	Kodanad	39
37.	Cheraman Juma Masjid, Kodungalloor	39
38.	Thrissur Pooram	41
39.	Guruvayoor	41
40.	Kerala Kalamandalam	43
41.	Punnathoorkotta	43
42.	Athirapally and Vazhachal	45
43.	Shakthan Thampuran Palace	45
44.	Jain Temple, Palakkad	47
45.	Nelliyampathy	47
46.	Aruvacode	49
47.	Kappad Beach	49
48.	Thamarassery Churam	51
49.	Wayanad Wildlife Sanctuary	51
50.	Ambalavayal Heritage Museum, Wayanad	52

Contents

51.	Edakkal Caves	52
52.	Makhdoom Palli, Ponnani	53
53.	Thunchan Parambu, Tirur	53
54.	Pookot Lake	54
55.	St. Angelos Fort, Kannur	54
56.	Thalassery Fort	55
57.	Gundert Bungalow	55
58.	Bekal Fort	57
59.	Malik Ibn Dinar Mosque	57
60.	Ananthapuram Lake Temple	59
61.	Kuttichira Mosque	59
62.	KIRTADS Ethnological Museum	59
63.	Mannar	61
64.	Onam	61
65.	River Nila (Bharatapuzha)	63
66.	Anayoottu	63
67.	Aranmula Kannadi	65
68.	Chundan Vallam (Snake Boat)	65
69.	Abhyangasnana	67
70.	Panchakarma	67
71.	Houseboats	69
72.	Festivals of Kerala	69
73.	Kathakali	73
74.	Mohiniyattam	73
75.	Kutiyattam	75

Contents

76.	Theyyam	75
77.	Chenda	78
78.	Panchavadyam	79
79.	Koothambalam	79
80.	Velichappadu	82
81.	Astrology	83
82.	Nilavilakku	83
83.	River Kabini	83
84.	Kanikonna	87
85.	Nalukettu	87
86.	Nettippattom	89
87.	Coir Products	89
88.	Uru	89
89.	Murals	91
90.	Sadya – Traditional Kerala Feast	91
91.	Monsoon	91
92.	Kasavu Mundu	94
93.	Spices of Kerala	95
94.	Kurumulaku (Black Pepper)	96
95.	Karicku (Tender Coconut)	97
96.	Kadumanga	98
97.	Kappa and Meen Curry (Tapioca and Fish Curry)	99
98.	Ada Pradhaman	100
99.	Parippuvada	101
100.	Kanji (Rice gruel)	102
101.	Chips	103

T.K.A. Nair

FOREWORD

*"The good, supreme, divine poetry of nature is above all rules and reason,
Whoever discerns its beauty with a firm, sedate gaze does not see it,
any more than he sees God Incarnate,
Such inherent beauty does not persuade our judgement,
it ravishes and overwhelms it."*

Legend has it that standing on the mountains Lord Parashurama threw an axe far into the sea and commanded the sea to retreat and a land richly endowed by nature emerged from the waters – a land that came to be called Kerala and more aptly, 'God's Own Country'.

Flanked by the Arabian Sea on the west and the towering Western Ghats on the east, Kerala is a long stretch of enchanting greenery with tall exotic coconut palms, dense tropical forests, farms, fertile plains, rocky coasts, beaches, an intricate maze of backwaters, still bays and an incredible network of forty-four rivers. Spread over 2,491 sq. kms this land of spices, tea, cashew nuts and rubber has attracted people from time immemorial resulting in an exotic history that merges with the epic Ramayana. The history of Kerala is replete with visits from the Far East, from ancient Persia as well as from the Roman Empire – it is believed that St. Thomas, one of the Apostles of Jesus Christ set foot on this land at the ancient port of Muziris (present – day Kodungalloor) – by Marco Polo, the Arab traders and later by the Portuguese Vasco da Gama who landed at Kappad in Calicut in AD 1498, followed by the Dutch and then the British. They came to the shores of Kerala after hearing of its rich treasures of spices and ivory, leaving behind a part of their customs and culture that the people assimilated and made their own. Little wonder then that this ancient haven so sought after by travellers is still a favourite destination for tourists from all over the world.

But travel, tourism and natural beauty are not reasons why people have been attracted to this magic land. Great learning in ancient scriptures, the ancient science of healing and rejuvenation, Ayurveda, the socio-religious reforms that were far ahead of their time and the post-independence achievements in the fields of education – Kerala boasts an almost 100 per cent literacy rate – public health and land reforms have drawn people to study what has come to be known as the 'Kerala Model'. A modern, vibrant, democratic State where women outnumber men (male to female ratio is 1:1.07). Kerala is repeatedly cited by many economists, and political scientists, Nobel Laureate Amartya Sen included, as a classic example of how socio-economic reforms coupled with equitable land reforms, stress on education, public health and a good public distribution system can bring forth the latent energies of the entire populace to push the pace of socio-economic development.

Another fascinating facet of this land is the character of the people that populate it. The hard working Keralites are highly adaptable and have often migrated in large numbers to the West and South East Asia – first to South East Asia and to Burma (present-day Myanmar), then to what is today Iran and then to the Middle East in search of employment, income and fortune, braving the risks of leaving the safety and comfort of their homeland for the rigours of a foreign environment. Today the professionals of Kerala are among the most wanted in the fields of medicine, information technology, tourism, teaching and nursing the world over. History has helped Keralites to develop a cosmopolitan outlook and their entrepreneurial skills and a can do attitude that has seen them prosper in the harshest environment. A visible sign of the highly mobile population is the presence of three international airports – at Thiruvananthapuram, Kochi and Kozhikode – a fairly developed and extensive network of motorable roads connecting different parts of the state, a railway system that passes through almost all of its fourteen districts and a large network of inland waterways.

A land of rivers, backwaters, coconut trees and blessed by a wide variety of flora and fauna, Kerala harbours significant biodiversity which includes tropical wet evergreen and semi-evergreen forests, tropical moist and dry deciduous forest, and montane subtropical and temperate (sholay) forests. Living in these lush green forests are the Asian elephant, Bengal tiger, leopard, nilgiri tahr, common palm civet, grizzled giant squirrel and a variety of reptiles including the king cobra, viper, python and crocodile. Kerala's birds are legion – Peafowl, the Great Hornbill (Buceros bicornis), Indian Grey Hornbill, Indian Cormorant, and Jungle Myna are several emblematic species. This diverse and delicate eco-system enjoys a climate that is mainly wet and maritime tropical, heavily influenced by the seasonal heavy rains brought by the Southwest Summer Monsoon and the North/west rains in winter months. As a result, Kerala averages 120-140 rainy days a year with the rains feeding its several rivers and streams that are the mainstay of its cash-crop agriculture.

Kerala is the land of Kalarippayattu, the ancient martial art said to be the precursor of Karate, Ju Jitsu and Kung Fu, that was carried to the Far East by Buddhist monks and which is still kept alive by enthusiasts from all over the world. The variety and the richness of the culture of Kerala are reflected in the many forms of dance and performing arts like Kathakali, Mohiniyattam, Thiruvathirakali, Kolkali, Oppana, Velakali, Chavittunatakom and Tholpavakoothu.

Despite its varied and colourful history and socio-cultural changes through the ages, modern-day Kerala still retains its traditions and customs, its cuisine and its culture, while it steps boldly into the 21st century, proud of its past and confident of its future. No wonder then that this most acclaimed destination of the Millennium and one of the top fifty must-visit-in-a-lifetime place according to the National Geographic Magazine continues to entice and charm all those who visit it.

INVIS Multimedia, the pioneers in digital content creation on Kerala and Indian heritage and systems of knowledge provides in the pages that follow in this beautifully brought out product invaluable insights into the USP of Kerala. Extracting the essence of the legendary Kerala is indeed a daunting task, yet this endeavour of INVIS deserves a hearty pat on the back for its authenticity, its textual and visual richness and its absorbing ethnic flavour. But what truly distinguishes this book is the 'human touch' imparted to the concept which stays with you long after you have turned the last leaf of it.

Now let INVIS lead you to discover your own paradise in God's Own Country!

Mr. T.K.A. Nair, Principal Secretary to Prime Minister of India is a former Secretary to Govt. of India, Ministry of Environment & Forests. His observations in this piece are entirely personal.

Padmanabha Swamy Temple

Padmanabha Swamy Temple

A majestic example of temple architecture towering over the heart of Thiruvananthapuram, to which the capital city owes its name. A magnificent blend of Kerala and Dravidian styles of architecture, the temple is renowned for its murals and lofty stone carvings. Only Hindus are allowed into the temple. Anybody can visit the interesting surroundings.

Open: 0415 - 0515 hrs, 0645 - 0730 hrs 0830 - 1030 hrs, 1130 - 1145 hrs, 1715 - 1930 hrs.
Dress code: Men – Dhoti. Women – Sari and blouse.
District : Thiruvananthapuram
Nearest railway station: Thiruvananthapuram Central, about 1 km away.
Nearest airport: Thiruvananthapuram International Airport, about 6 kms away.

Padmanabhapuram Palace

This magnificent palace of the Rajas of the erstwhile Kingdom of Travancore (AD 1550 to 1750) is an enticing sight to any lover of art and architecture in wood. Though the palace is presently in the Kanyakumari district of the neighbouring state of Tamil Nadu, it is owned and maintained by the Government of Kerala. One of the biggest wooden palaces in the world, this is a monument not to be missed.

Open: 0900 hrs- 1300 hrs, 1400 hrs- 1630 hrs.
Closed on Mondays, January 26th, May 1st, August 15th, Thiruvonam and October 2nd.
District : Kanyakumari, Tamil Nadu
Nearest railway stations: Eraniyal, about 6 kms away and Nagarcoil, about 20 kms away.
Nearest airport: Thiruvananthapuram International Airport, about 70 kms away.

Kovalam

Kovalam

The golden sand crescent beaches where the Indian Ocean is at its aquaserene best. The tropical sun, the calm waters, palm fronds waving in the sea breeze, hibiscus blooms in the moonlit nights and the faint murmur of the surf are all part of the magic of Kovalam. Kovalam now is a year round favourite destination since the monsoon season too has started attracting monsoon chasing tourists.

District : Thiruvananthapuram
Nearest railway station: Thiruvananthapuram Central, about 16 kms away.
Nearest airport: Thiruvananthapuram International Airport, about 10 kms away.

Varkala

A quiet sea resort, rich in mineral water springs; Varkala is considered a holy beach. The two thousand year old shrine of the Janardhanaswamy (Sri Krishna) temple stands as a timeless monument as eternal as the sea. The Sivagiri Mutt, founded by the great Hindu reformer and philosopher Sree Narayana Guru (1856 - 1928) is close by.

District : Thiruvananthapuram
Nearest railway station: Varkala, about 2 kms away.
Nearest airport: Thiruvananthapuram International Airport, about 45 kms away.

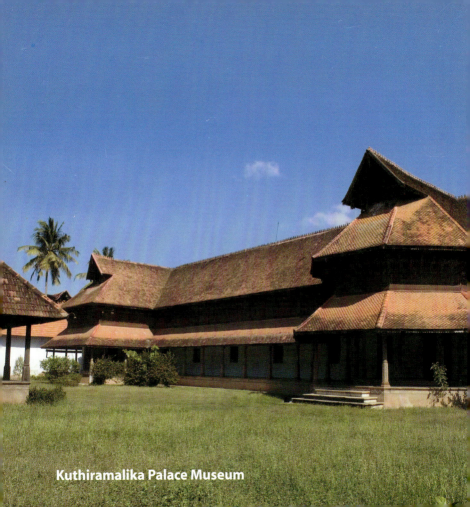
Kuthiramalika Palace Museum

Kuthiramalika Palace Museum

The Kuthiramalika Palace adjacent to the Padmanabha Swamy Temple is a must stopover for anyone who takes pleasure in exquisite wood carving, historic paintings and priceless heirlooms of a bygone era. Built by the poet, musician and social reformer king of Travancore, Maharaja Swathi Thirunal Balarama Varma, the airy palace is a rare monument in the heart of the capital city.

District : Thiruvananthapuram
Open: 0830-0100 hrs & 1500- 1730 hrs. Closed on Mondays.
Nearest railway station: Thiruvananthapuram Central, about 1 km away.
Nearest airport: Thiruvananthapuram International Airport, about 6 kms away.

Sree Chithra Art Gallery

A treasure trove for the art lover, the Sree Chithra Art Gallery is located in the beautiful Napier museum and zoo complex in Thiruvananthapuram city. You can see the famed paintings of Raja Ravi Varma. The museum also houses exquisite works from the Rajput, Mughal and Tanjore schools of art.

District : Thiruvananthapuram
Open: 1000-1645 hrs. Closed on Mondays and Wednesday forenoons.
Nearest railway station: Thiruvananthapuram Central, about 3 kms away.
Nearest airport: Thiruvananthapuram International Airport, about 9 kms away.

Kutiyattam performance at Margi

Valiya Koyikkal Palace

Valiya Koyikkal Palace, Nedumangadu, east of the capital city, is a typical example of the traditional Kerala architecture. The palace is built in the famous *Nalukettu* style. Today the palace houses a numismatics museum and a folklore museum. Margi Kathakali Centre near Fort High School

District : Thiruvananthapuram
Open: 0900 hrs to 1630 hrs. Closed on Mondays.
Nearest railway station: Thiruvananthapuram Central, about 18 kms away.
Nearest airport: Thiruvananthapuram International Airport, about 24 kms away.

Margi

For any tourist with even a cursory interest in Kerala's diverse cultural bouquet, Margi is a one stop destination to savour the flavours of a classical art feast. Established in 1970, Margi has two centres in Thiruvananthapuram city, one near Fort High School behind the Padmanabha Swamy temple, solely for Kathakali and another near the Valiyasala temple for Kutiyattam and Koothu. In addition to the regular monthly programmes performances will be staged if booked in advance.

Margi Kathakali Centre near Fort High School
Nearest railway station: Thiruvananthapuram Central, about 2 kms away.
Nearest airport: Thiruvananthapuram International Airport, about 6 kms away.
Margi Kutiyattam Centre near Valiyasala Temple
Nearest railway station: Thiruvananthapuram Central, about 2 kms away.
Nearest airport: Thiruvananthapuram International Airport, about 8 kms away .

Kalarippayattu

Kalarippayattu

Kalarippayattu is Kerala's own martial art form. Any martial art lover must see the intricate blend of physical prowess, mental agility and perfection in martial techniques that gives a captivating style to this form of armed, close quarter, hand-to- hand combat. The Kalari is a practice ring and Payattu denotes the various combats trained in it. Kalarippayattu duels are fought using swords, sticks, spears, daggers and even a whip like springy long sword called Urumi. There are two schools of Kalarippayattu, the north Kerala version and the south Kerala one. Both have evolved their own brands of indigenous herbal medicines and treatments which work wonders for cuts, sprains and fractures.

Some Kalari centres:

CVN Kalari, Thiruvananthapuram
Nearest railway station: Thiruvananthapuram Central, about 1 km away.
Nearest airport: Thiruvananthapuram International Airport, about 6 kms away.

Indian School of Martial Arts, Thiruvananthapuram
Nearest railway station: Thiruvananthapuram Central, about 2 kms away.
Nearest airport: Thiruvananthapuram International Airport, about 9 kms away.

Athreya Ayurvedic Centre, Kottayam
Nearest railway station: Kottayam, about 5 kms away.
Nearest airport: Cochin International Airport, about 80 kms away.

CVN Kalari, Kozhikode
Nearest railway station: Kozhikode, about 2 kms away.
Nearest airport : Karipur Airport, about 25 kms from Kozhikode.

Kuttanad - backwater life

Palaruvi Waterfalls

Literally meaning the brook or rivulet of milk, Palaruvi, one of the major waterfalls in south India is a mesmerising sight to behold. As the milky white foaming water cascades 90 metres down between the rocks it drenches visitors in a cool spray. The best season to visit the waterfall is between June and January.

District : Kollam
Nearest railway station: Kollam, about 60 kms away.
Nearest airport: Thiruvananthapuram International Airport, about 80 kms away.

Kuttanad

Kuttanad is one of the great wonders in the magic that Kerala weaves. Formerly the 'rice bowl' of the state, Kuttanad is virtually a vast waterlogged area below sea level in central Kerala. You can enter Kuttanad from various places in Alappuzha, Kottayam and Pathanamthitta districts. Plush houseboats are available for hire.

Nearest railway station: Alappuzha.
Nearest airport: Cochin International Airport, about 85 kms from Alappuzha.

Attukal Pongala

One day in a year, around February - March, women pilgrims congregate at a temple devoted to Goddess Bhagavathi at Attukal, a few kms south of Padmanabha Swamy temple in Thiruvananthapuram. They carry dried coconut spathes and fronds for making a fire, rice, molasses and condiments to make a sweet offering called *Pongala*. This is said to be the largest single gathering of women anywhere.

District : Thiruvananthapuram
Nearest railway station : Thiruvananthapuram Central, about 4 kms away.
Nearest airport : Thiruvananthapuram International Airport, about 8 kms away.

Thenmala Eco- tourism

Thenmala – a small village, surrounded by thick forests at the foothills of the Western Ghats has today become the venue of the first eco-tourism project in the state. Days long itinaries which include river boating, nature trail, river bank treks to waterfalls and adventure activity like mountain biking and rock climbing are available.

District : Kollam
Nearest railway station: Kollam, about 60 kms away.
Nearest airport: Thiruvananthapuram International Airport, about 70 kms away.

Mannarasala Nagaraja Temple

Sacred groves with serpent shrines in them have been an integral part of traditional Hindu households and villages of Kerala since time immemorial. Mannarasala is the most famous and largest serpent shrine of Kerala. The rituals are performed by the eldest female member of the clan here.

District : Alappuzha
Nearest railway station: Harippad, about 4 kms away.
Nearest airport: Cochin International Airport, about 100 kms away.

Krishnapuram Palace

Replete with gabled roofs, inner courtyards, dormer windows and rare artefacts, the palace is a protected monument under the Archaeology Department. It is also an archaeological museum. For the art lover there is a rare bonanza, a 49 square metre single band of mural painting – *Gajendra Moksham* – the largest of its kind discovered so far in Kerala.

District : Alappuzha
Open: Tuesday to Sunday, 0900 hrs to 1630 hrs.
Nearest railway stations: Kayamkulam, about 3 kms away and Kollam, about 39 kms away.
Nearest airport: Thiruvananthapuram International Airport, about 97 kms away.

Nehru Trophy Boat Race

Nehru Trophy Boat Race

One of the most thrilling races in the world set on the magnificent waterscape of the backwaters of central Kerala. As the majestic snake boats or *Chundanvallams*, nearly 100 feet in length, with raised sterns resembling the rearing hood of snakes, surge ahead, neck-to-neck, one gets a glimpse of the harnessing of human spirit and prowess. Conducted on the second Saturday of August every year, this race is the pride of Kerala.

District : Alappuzha
Nearest railway station: Alappuzha, about 8 kms away.
Nearest airport: Cochin International Airport, about 85 kms from Alappuzha.

Niranam Church

An ancient monument considered to be one among the sacred seven-and-a-half churches originally established in AD 52 by St. Thomas who is believed to have come to Kerala. The tall granite cross in front of the church dates back to AD 1259 and is a proud relic of the past. Antique carvings, murals and sculptures make this place interesting.

District : Pathanamthitta
Nearest railway station: Thiruvalla, about 9 kms away.
Nearest airport: Cochin International Airport, about 110 kms away.

Champakkulam Kalloorkadu Church

Champakkulam Kalloorkadu Church

For the history buff and the devout, this magnificent church on the banks of river Pampa and steeped in history is a place worth visiting. Built in AD 427 and renovated first in 1730 and later in 1891, this architectural tribute to time is an imposing structure set amidst Kuttanad's picturesque waterscape.

District : Alappuzha
Nearest railway stations: Changanasserry, about 20 kms away and Alappuzha, about 24 kms away.
Nearest airport: Cochin International Airport, about 85 kms from Alappuzha.

Patayani

This spectacular ritual art form lasting from five to twenty-eight days is performed in the *Devi* or mother Goddess temples in Pathanamthitta and surroundings. *Pata* means army and *Ani*, the ranks, this dance form was once believed to prepare the clan for war. Patayani is performed mostly in the December to April months when most temple festivals occur. The Neelamperoor Patayani is staged during the Onam (August – September) season.

Vastu Vidya Gurukulam & Vijnana Kalavedi, Aranmula

Vastu Vidya Gurukulam

Vastu Vidya Gurukulam is an autonomous institution under the State Cultural Affairs Department for the promotion of traditional architecture and mural paintings. It has also been selected as the implementing agency for the Endogenous Tourism Programme (ETP) of the Union Government and the United Nations Development Programme (UNDP) to support Aranmula's local culture, economy and social life. The Gurukulam offers consultancy services in Vastu Vidya or the traditional architecture.

Vijnana Kalavedi

A centre providing a rare facility – an opportunity to acquaint yourself with the culture and arts of Kerala. If you are an artist, researcher or culture tourist, Vijnana Kalavedi is a one stop destination to stay and learn more about the traditions of this land. Founded by Ms. Louba Schild, an artist from France who has made Kerala her home since 1968, the centre was declared by the Department of Culture, Govt. of Kerala as a cultural education institution engaged in the teaching and promotion of traditional arts and Indian culture. Vijnana Kalavedi attempts to preserve the traditional arts and crafts of Kerala in their natural and spiritual context and also foster art education among the youth in the state. Visitors from all over the world are welcome for short or long - term stay to learn about local art forms.

District : Pathanamthitta
Nearest railway station: Chengannur, about 11 kms away.
Nearest airports: Thiruvananthapuram International Airport and Cochin International Airport, both about 140 kms away.

Sabarimala

A phenomenon among pilgrimages. Nestling some 1000 metres above sea level on the mountain ranges of the Western Ghats, this shrine to Lord Ayyappa is surrounded by thick forest and is accessible only by foot from the Pamba river. Open only the first five days of every Malayalam month, the main pilgrimage season falls around mid November to late December. Mandala Pooja and Makaravilakku the two main events occur then. The devotees take strict celibate vows and practice an austere vegetarian diet for 41 days as a penance before the pilgrimage. They wear black and carry on their heads bundled offerings like coconuts filled with ghee. Women after their menarche and before the menopause are not allowed to make the trip since Lord Ayyappa is a celibate. The sight of thousands of black clad men, climbing the hills after a dip in the holy Pampa, chanting Lord Ayyappa's name in unison fills one with a sense of metaphysical wonder – at the human craving to become one with the supreme. The pilgrimage's popularity now transcends the state's borders.

Open: Pilgrim season: November to mid January. Also open in the first five days of every Malayalam month and during Vishu (April).

Road transport is only available up to Pamba, which is about 65 kms from Pathanamthitta. From there one has to walk a distance of 4 kms.

District : Pathanamthitta

Nearest railway Station: Chengannur, about 28 kms from Pathanamthitta. You can also go by road from Kottayam or Thiruvalla railway station.

Nearest airport: Thiruvananthapuram International Airport, about 130 kms from Chengannur.

St. Thomas Church, Kodungalloor

Kodungalloor situated 35 kilometres south of Thrissur, on the west coast, was once a great port of the Chera rulers of Tamil Nadu. Christ's apostle St.Thomas is believed to have landed at Kodungalloor in 52 AD. The St.Thomas Church established by him here houses ancient relics. He had preached the gospel from Ethiopia to China. At Kodungalloor, St.Thomas established the first Christian church in India.

District : Thrissur
Nearest railway station: Irinjalakuda, about 20 kms away.
Nearest airport: Cochin International Airport, about 50 kms away.

Kumarakom

This is an unbelievably beautiful paradise of mangrove forests, emerald paddy fields and coconut groves interspersed with placid waterways and canals lined with white lilies. The village of Kumarakom is spread over a cluster of little islands on the Vembanad Lake and is part of the Kuttanad region. The bird sanctuary here, which is spread across 14 acres, is a favourite haunt of migratory birds and is an ornithologist's paradise.

District : Kottayam
Nearest railway station: Kottayam, about 16 kms away.
Nearest airport: Cochin International Airport, about 95 kms away.

Muniyara

Muniyara, Marayoor

An awe inspiring sight here is the timeless mountains standing guard over the solemn relics of time, the Muniyaras, pre-historic stone burial chambers. Historians call them dolmenoids or burial cists, made up of four stones placed on edges and covered by a huge stone on top called the cap stone.

Marayoor-Munnar is 40 km and Munnar-Idukki is 55 kms by road.
District : Idukki
Nearest railway station: Ernakulam, about 145 kms from Munnar.
Nearest airport: Cochin International Airport, about 110 kms from Munnar.

Periyar Wildlife Sanctuary

The Periyar Wildlife Sanctuary is situated on the banks of the Periyar Lake, Thekkady. You can see herds of wild elephants, deer, bison, boars and other animals come down to the lake's edge for a drink.

Open: 0600 to 1800 hrs.
District : Idukki
Nearest railway station: Kottayam, about 114 kms from Thekkady.
Nearest airport: Cochin International Airport, about 190 kms from Thekkady.

Periyar Wildlife Sanctuary

Eravikulam National Park

A haven for the rare and endangered Nilgiri Tahr, a mountain goat species. Eravikulam National Park is a beautiful natural preserve. Anamudi, the highest peak (2695 ms) south of the Himalayas, rises like a citadel over the park. An ideal place for trekkers.

Open: 0800- 1700 hrs. Visitors not allowed during monsoon season.
Eravikulam is 15 kms away from Munnar.
District : Idukki
Nearest railway station: Ernakulam, about 145 kms from Munnar.
Nearest airport: Cochin International Airport, about 110 kms from Munnar.

Munnar

The mist wreathed Munnar nestling 1600 metres above sea level at the confluence of three mountain streams – Mudrapuzha, Nallathanni and Kundala – is one of the most popular tourist paradises in India. The cool mountain air of the high ranges, the green magic of nature, tinkling streams and little waterfalls that you stumble upon on the wayside, all make Munnar a memorable experience.
Munnar is accessible by road from Ernakulam and Kottayam.

District : Idukki
Nearest railway station: Ernakulam, about 145 kms away.
Nearest airport: Cochin International Airport, about 110 kms away.

Eravikulam National Park

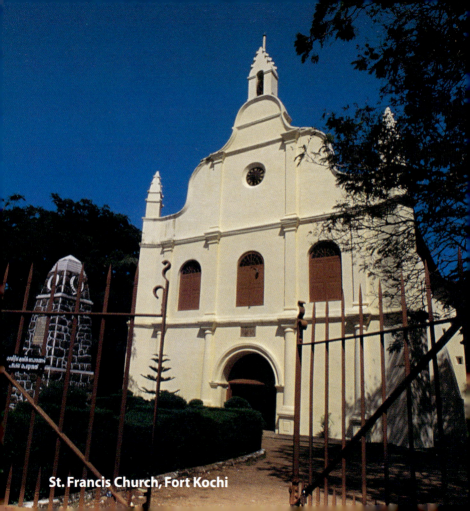
St. Francis Church, Fort Kochi

Hill Palace Museum, Thripunithura

Kerala's first heritage museum, it houses the royal collections of the erstwhile Kochi kingdom. Built in 1865, the palace complex has a collection of the finest specimens of traditional architecture of Kerala along with a collection of priceless antiques, murals, sculptures, coins and inscriptions.

Open: 0900- 1630 hrs; Children's Park: 0900- 1800 hrs. Closed on Mondays.
District : Ernakulam
Nearest railway station: Ernakulam, about 10 kms away.
Nearest airport: Cochin International Airport, about 33 kms away.

Fort Kochi

A fine way to know Kochi would be a walking tour of the old streets of Fort Kochi. A haven for people from all over the world, Kochi was the first European township in India as the Portuguese settled here in the 15th century. Walking through Fort Kochi, you come across interesting sights like the Chinese fishing nets along the Vasco da Gama Square, Santa Cruz Basilica, St. Francis Church, VOC Gate and the Bastion Bungalow.

District : Ernakulam
Nearest railway station: Ernakulam, about 16 kms away.
Nearest airport: Cochin International Airport, about 40 kms away.

Jew Street

The first Jewish settlements of the subcontinent were in Kerala and Kochi boasted of the biggest settlement. Even though all but a handful of Jews from Kochi have left for Israel, the Jewish Synagogue, a monument of exceptional architectural beauty and history draws hundreds of people to its portals everyday.

District : Ernakulam
Nearest railway station: Ernakulam, about 16 kms away.
Nearest airport: Cochin International Airport, about 40 kms away.

Mattancherry Palace

A gift from the coloniser to the colonised, the Mattancherry Palace was built by the Portuguese in 1557 and presented to Raja Veera Kerala Varma of Kochi. The magnificent structure replete with a Goddess Bhagavathi temple in the central courtyard is a proud example of the Kerala style mansion or *Nalukettu*. The double storeyed palace building which stands by the panoramic Kochi backwaters has an exquisite collection of murals covering over 300 square feet of its walls.

Open: 1000- 1700 hrs. Closed on Fridays.
There are frequent bus and boat services to Mattancherry. The boats start from the main boat jetty near Subhash Park in Ernakulam town.
District : Ernakulam
Nearest railway station: Ernakulam, about 16 kms away.
Nearest airport: Cochin International Airport, about 40 kms away.

Chinese Fishing Nets

Chinese Fishing Nets

Bowl shaped Chinese fishing nets dipping slowly into the tranquil backwaters in the glow of the setting sun – this is a scene that has become the hallmark of Kochi. They were brought to this land by Chinese traders. A fascinating mechanism, these nets are lowered into the water mostly after sundown and a lamp in the middle attracts the fish in the dark backwaters.

District : Ernakulam
Nearest railway station: Ernakulam, about 16 kms away.
Nearest airport: Cochin International Airport, about 40 kms away.

Malayattoor Church

Declared by the Vatican as an international pilgrim centre, this ancient church atop the Malayattoor hill nestles in the imposing Kodanad ranges. Dedicated to St. Thomas, the apostle of Jesus Christ, thousands of pilgrims gather here for the annual festival of Malayattoor Perunnal held during the months of March /April.

District : Ernakulam
Nearest railway station: Angamali, about 30 kms away.
Nearest airport: Cochin International Airport, about 25 kms away.

Indo – Portuguese Museum, Kochi

A monument to the confluence of Indian and Portuguese cultures, this museum displays some of the most glorious moments in the history of Kochi. An important centre to study Indo-Portuguese Christian art heritage, the museum is divided into five main sections, namely – altar, treasure, procession, civil life and cathedral. It currently houses some outstanding collections.

District : Ernakulam
Nearest railway station: Ernakulam, about 16 kms away.
Nearest airport: Cochin International Airport, about 40 kms away.

Chennamangalam Synagogue

This is a 175-year-old synagogue built by the Jews who settled at Chennamangalam nearly two centuries ago. Chennamangalam shot to fame owing to the synagogue, an imposing blend of native and colonial architecture. The synagogue remains intact even though like in Kochi most Jews have departed to settle in their promised land, Israel.

District : Ernakulam
Nearest railway station: Aluva, about 25 kms away.
Nearest airport: Cochin International Airport, about 33 kms away.

Kodanad

In earlier days, elephants were trapped regularly from the forests in annual drives, to be trained and domesticated at the training centres. Now there is a ban on elephant trapping. However, the forest authorities do get a few elephants, especially babies from the forests, washed down in mountain floods or whose mothers have died. The elephant training centre at Kodanad on the banks of river Periyar amidst the mountain ranges offers interesting sights.

District : Ernakulam
Nearest railway station: Angamali, about 25 kms away.
Nearest airport: Cochin International Airport, about 20 kms away.

Cheraman Juma Masjid, Kodungalloor

Built by the first Islamic missionary to Kerala, Malik Ibn Dinar in AD 629, it is believed to be the first mosque on the Indian subcontinent. This mosque too is at the site of the ancient port of Kodungalloor. The mosque is built in traditional Kerala architectural style.

District : Thrissur
Nearest railway station: Irinjalakkuda, about 16 kms away.
Nearest airport: Cochin International Airport, about 45 kms away.

Thrissur Pooram

The festival of festivals and grand bonanza of colours, lights, massed native drums and horns plus magnificent elephant pageantry, the Thrissur Pooram shouldn't be missed. Pooram normally falls between 15th April and 15th May. Even though the major event is a one day affair, the festivities begin around ten days prior to this. On the final day, the deities set out in all regalia on caparisoned elephants to the Pooram ground in front of the city centre Vadakkumnatha temple. The *Pakal* Pooram (daylight Pooram) staged the next morning is a recap of the main Pooram's highlights.

District : Thrissur
Nearest railway station: Thrissur, about 1 km away.
Nearest airport: Cochin International Airport, about 55 kms away.

Guruvayoor

The Lord Krishna temple at Guruvayoor attracts thousands of devotees from all parts of India. Only Hindus are allowed to enter the premises of this ancient temple. Krishnanattam, a classical dance drama portraying the story of Lord Krishna is regularly performed as a ritual offering here inside the temple premises. There is also a Krishnanattam training centre outside the temple where tourists can see the dance form being taught.

District : Thrissur
Nearest railway stations: Guruvayoor, about 1km and Thrissur, about 30 kms away.
Nearest airport: Cochin International Airport, about 80 kms away.

Kerala Kalamandalam

Established in 1930, Kerala Kalamandalam, near Shornur is a centre of excellence for training in Kerala's performing arts, especially Kathakali, the classical dance form. Kathakali music and percussion instruments needed for the performance of these art forms are also taught here. There are long-term and short-term courses.

District : Thrissur
Nearest railway station: Shornur, about 10 kms away.
Nearest airport : Cochin International Airport, about 85 kms away.

Punnathoorkotta

The biggest centre for domesticated elephants in the world, over 60 jumbos are housed here. Owned by the Guruvayoor temple, the centre rears elephants donated to the temple as ritual offerings by devotees. An interesting ritual here is called *Aanayoottu* when devotees and jumbo fans feed the elephants with giant boluses of boiled and sweetened rice and bananas.

Open: 0800 hrs to 1800 hrs on all days.
District : Thrissur
Nearest railway station: Guruvayoor, about 3 kms away.
Nearest airport: Cochin International Airport, about 85 kms away.

Athirapally

Athirapally and Vazhachal

The most scenic waterfalls of Kerala, they are just 5 kilometres apart from each other. Their beauty attracts thousands of visitors every year. To get drenched in the cool spray of Athirapally fall tumbling down nearly 24 metres is an exhilarating experience. The motorable forest roads to these falls are misty and picturesque.

A good motorable road takes you to Vazhachal and Athirapally from either Kochi or Thrissur town.
District : Thrissur
Nearest railway station: Thrissur, about 63 kms away.
Nearest airport: Cochin International Airport, about 115 kms away.

Shakthan Thampuran Palace

This ancient palace in Thrissur originally known as Vadakkechira Kovilakam was renovated by Rama Varma Shaktan Thampuran (1751 – 1805) who ruled the erstwhile princely state of Kochi. Hence it became popular as the Shakthan Thampuran Palace. Recently the state Archaeology Department converted it into an archaeology museum.

District : Thrissur
Nearest railway station: Thrissur, about 2 kms away.
Nearest airport: Cochin International Airport, about 55 kms away.

Nelliyampathy

Jain Temple, Palakkad

The Jain monuments of Kerala may be grouped under two categories: rock shelters and structural temples. One of the major Jain temples remaining is in the western suburb of Palakkad town. The place is known as Jainamedu. The 32 feet long 20 feet wide granite temple displays images of the Jain Theerthankaras and Yakshinis.

District : Palakkad
Nearest railway station: Palakkad, about 2 kms away.
Nearest airport: Cochin International Airport, about 100 kms away.

Nelliyampathy

The road to Nelliyampathy hill station has about ten hairpin bends and offers a breathtaking view of the evergreen forests. From certain points of the road you can see vast stretches of the Palakkad district. Nelliyampathy is an ideal retreat for the nature enthusiast with avenues open for trekking and wildlife observation.

District : Palakkad
Nearest railway station: Palakkad, about 75 kms away.
Nearest airport: Cochin International Airport, about 150 kms away.

Aruvacode

Aruvacode is a small village in north Kerala famous for its potters. The villagers here found it difficult to survive, with the influx of cheap industrial substitutes. An activist- designer came forward to re-engineer their skills. Together they explored the possibilities of terra-cotta suited to the modern context.

District : Malappuram
Nearest railway station: Nilambur, about 5 kms away.
Nearest airport: Karipur Airport, about 35 kms away.

Kappad Beach

On May 20, 1498, 170 men led by Portuguese navigator Vasco da Gama (1469 – 1524) landed at this beach and it was the beginning of a long and tumultuous socio-political relationship between India and Europe. There is a temple believed to be 800 years old on the nearby rocks. A journey between Kozhikode and Kappad through the backwaters is an unforgettable experience.

The best route to Kappad is along the bewitching backwaters. A ride down the backwaters through the Korappuzha river brings you to the beach.
District : Kozhikode
Nearest railway station: Kozhikode, about 16 kms away.
Nearest airport: Karipur Airport, about 39 kms away.

Thamarassery churam

Thamarassery churam is a mountain pass at an elevation of 700 metres above sea level. It connects Kozhikode with Wayanad, which is one of the most beautiful and least explored districts of the state. The one hour trip up the 12 kms road with hairpin bends amidst thick forested slopes is a fascinating experience.

Nearest railway station: Kozhikode, about 50 kms away.
Nearest airport: Karipur Airport, about 73 kms away.

Wayanad Wildlife Sanctuary

Established in 1973, the Wayanad Wildlife Sanctuary is a part of the protected area network of Nagarhole and Bandipur in the neighbouring State of Karnataka on the northeast and Mudumalai in the neighbouring state of Tamil Nadu on the southeast. The sanctuary is very rich in flora and fauna.

Open: 0800 hrs to 1700 hrs
District : Wayanad
Nearest railway station: Kozhikode, about 97 kms from Sulthan Bathery.
Nearest airport: Karipur Airport, about 120 kms away.

Ambalavayal Heritage Museum, Wayanad

This Museum has one of Kerala's largest collections of the remnants of an era dating back to the 2nd century A.D. At the museum you can see articles as varied as clay sculptures, ancient hunting equipments like bows and arrows, stone weapons and other historical artefacts belonging to various tribes of the region.

Open: 1000 hrs to 1700 hrs
District : Wayanad
Nearest railway station: Kozhikode, about 97 kms from Sulthan Bathery.
Nearest airport: Karipur Airport, about 120 kms away.

Edakkal Caves

The Edakkal caves in the Ambukuthi Hills in north Kerala are considered to be one of the earliest centres of human habitation. Inside the caves you will find ancient stone scripts, pictorial wall inscriptions of human and animal figures, the swastik form, symbols and cave drawings of human figures and so on.

Open: Morning hours are ideal for the visit. Entry is permitted only till 1700 hrs.
Location: On Ambukuthi Mala, about 12 kms from Sulthan Bathery.
The caves can be reached either by a 5 kms trek from Ambalavayal or by a 1 km trekking trail from Edakkal.
District : Wayanad
Nearest railway station: Kozhikode railway station, about 97 kms from Sultan Bathery.
Nearest airport: Karipur Airport, about 120 kms away.

Makhdoom Palli, Ponnani

Situated at Ponnani, a coastal town of northern Kerala, Makhdoom Palli (Valiya Jum - A Masjid) is one of the oldest mosques of Kerala. Besides Keralites, people from distant places like Sumatra and Java are said to have come to Makhdoom Palli to study Islam. This mosque at Ponnani is a perfect tribute to Kerala's traditional style of architecture.

District : Malappuram
Nearest railway station: Tirur, about 30 kms away.
Nearest airport: Karipur Airport, about 75 kms away.

Thunchan Parambu, Tirur

Thunchathu Ezhuthachan is considered as the father of Malayalam, the language of the state of Kerala. The literary works of Ezhuthachan in the later half of 16th century gave Malayalam a philosophic depth, a new aesthetics and style unprecedented in the language. A memorial to this great scholar is built at Thunchan Parambu, his birthplace.

District : Malappuram
Nearest railway station: Tirur, about 1 km away.
Nearest airport: Karipur Airport, about 60 kms away.

Pookot Lake

A natural freshwater lake surrounded by evergreen forests and rolling hills at an altitude of 2100 metres above sea level. A freshwater aquarium with large variety of fish is an added attraction. Tourists can also avail of boating facilities, children's park and a shopping centre for handicrafts and spices.

District : Wayanad
Nearest railway station: Kozhikode, about 60 kms away.
Nearest airport: Karipur Airport, about 85 kms away.

St. Angelos Fort, Kannur

A massive triangular laterite fort, complete with a moat and flanking bastions, the St. Angelos Fort, also called Kannur Fort, was constructed in 1505. The spectacular view of the Moppila Bay and Dharmadom Island from the fort is indeed a rare opportunity to savour nature in the shade of history. Dharmadom, a beautiful five acre emerald island just 100 metres from the mainland is another place to dunk in the sea and soak in the sun.

District : Kannur
Nearest railway station: Kannur, about 3 kms away.
Nearest airport: Karipur Airport, about 85 kms from Kannur.

Thalassery Fort

Thalassery is a small town with its own imposing historical monument that towers over the place, the Thalassery Fort. The fort built in 1703 was once a hub of activity. The massive fort is a perfect choice for a historical holiday in the tropical coastline.

District : Kannur
Nearest railway station: Thalasseri, about 1.5 kms away.
Nearest airport: Karipur Airport, about 90 kms from Kannur.

Gundert Bungalow

Herman Gundert (1814 – 1893) was a German missionary and scholar who made great contributions to Malayalam language and literature. He spent two decades at Illikunnu Bungalow in Thalasseri, which houses his memorial today.
He wrote and published more than 25 books which includes the first Malayalam-English dictionary.

District : Kannur
Nearest railway station: Thalasseri, about 3 kms away.
Nearest airport: Karipur Airport, about 90 kms away.

Bekal Fort

Bekal Fort

Shaped like a giant keyhole, the historic Bekal fort offers a superb view of the Arabian Sea from its tall bastions from where a few centuries ago huge cannons commanded the waves. Constructed by the rulers of ancient Kadampa dynasty, the Bekal fort changed hands many times over the years to the Kolathiri Rajas, the Vijayanagar empire, Tipu Sultan and finally to the British East India.

District : Kasaragod
Nearest railway station: Kasaragod, about 16 kms away.
Nearest airports: Mangalore, about 85 kms away and Karipur Airport, about 200 kms away.

Malik Ibn Dinar Mosque

The first Islamic missionary to arrive in Kerala. The Malik Ibn Dinar mosque near Kasaragod, one of the oldest and most famous mosques of India, was built by Dinar's nephew. This is a three storeyed mosque built in the traditional Kerala architectural style

District : Kasaragod
Nearest railway station: Kasaragod, about 1 km away.
Nearest airports: Mangalore, about 70 kms away and Karipur Airport, about 200 kms away.

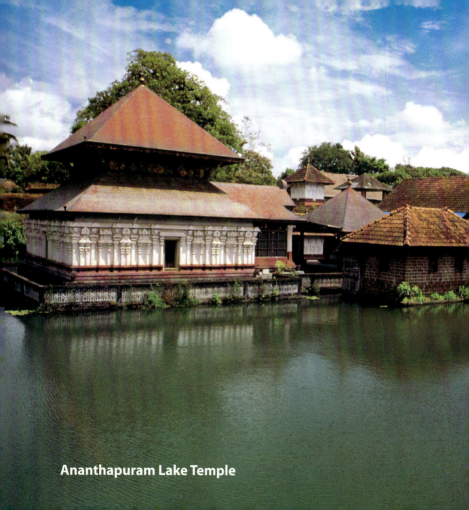
Ananthapuram Lake Temple

Ananthapuram Lake Temple

This 9th century temple near Kasaragod is the only lake temple in Kerala. Archaeologists estimate that the temple dates back to the 11th or 12th centuries. Surrounded by water on all sides the temple offers a riveting sight, as though it is hewn out of a single mammoth rock – a poem in laterite and wood.

District : Kasaragod
Nearest railway station: Kasaragod, about 13 kms away.
Nearest airports: Mangalore, about 80 kms away and Karipur Airport, about 200 kms away.

Kuttichira Mosque

The Jum-A Ath mosque is situated on the side of a lake in Kuttichira, Kozhikode town. The mosque, popularly known as Niskara Palli, finds mention in African travel writer Ibn Batuta's (AD 1304 – 1368) writings. The Jum-A Ath mosque is a four-storeyed structure built in accordance with traditional Kerala architecture.

District : Kozhikode
Nearest railway station: Kozhikode, about 1 km away.
Nearest airport: Karipur Airport, about 23 kms away.

KIRTADS Ethnological Museum

The Ethnological Museum established in 1973 is an interesting storehouse of information on the castes and tribes of Kerala. It houses a large collection of artefacts, costumes, jewellery, household utensils, nets and traps, wood carvings, agricultural tools, musical instruments and ceremonial paraphernalia of the earliest inhabitants of Kerala.

District : Kozhikode
Nearest railway station: Kozhikode, about 7 kms away.
Nearest airport: Karipur Airport, about 20 kms away.

Floral decoration during Onam

Mannar

A village on the Kayamkulam-Thiruvalla route, renowned for its cottage industry of bronze artefacts. A wide range of products like bells, lamps, vessels and kitchen utensils are available in attractive designs. An ancient Hindu temple, Panayannar Kavu, with one of the largest sacred groves and the Parumala Church are also near Mannar.

District : Alappuzha
Nearest railway station: Thiruvalla, about 13 kms away.
Nearest airport : Cochin International Airport, about 110 kms away.

Onam

Onam, the biggest festival of Kerala, is based on the evergreen myth of Mahabali, the emperor under whose rule this land enjoyed great prosperity and peace. Everyyear after harvest, around August or September the land decks up in anticipation of this beloved king's visit from the nether world. One can witness a number of festivals and cultural activities during the Onam days. The dates and the details of these festivals can be found in www.keralatourism.org.

River Nila (Bharatapuzha)

River Nila (Bharatapuzha)

River Nila, also known as Bharatapuzha, is the lifeline of Northern Kerala. Take a *thoni* (canoe) cruise which carries the traveller along the verdant banks of the river or go rafting which allows one to feel the river's flow. The River Nila is a world in itself, ideal for camping and viewing classical and folk-art performances.

Nearest railway station : Shornur, about 10 kms away.
Nearest airport : Cochin International Airport, about 85 kms away.

Anayoottu

Anayoottu, literally means 'feeding the elephant'. Many of the major temples of Kerala have domesticated elephants. Feeding an elephant is considered a holy ritual. You can conduct an *Anayoottu* by remitting the required fee at Punnathoorkotta, the elephant hostel of Guruvayoor temple. Aanayoottu on a grand scale is staged every year on the first day of the last Malayalam month of Karkkadakam (normally falling between July 10–18 every year) at the Vadakkumnatha temple, Thrissur.

Vadakkumnatha Temple

District : Thrissur
Nearest railway station : Thrissur, about 1 km away.
Nearest airport : Cochin International Airport, about 55 kms away.

Aranmula Kannadi

Aranmula Kannadi

A metal mirror dating from the days when even glass mirrors were unheard of, the Aranmula Kannadi (mirror from Aranmula) is mounted on an ornamental brass frame with a handle. While glass mirrors break, the metal Aranmula mirror lasts unbroken for generations. There is no refraction either. You can buy one at any reputed handicrafts shop.

District : Pathanamthitta
Nearest railway station: Chengannur, about 11 kms away.
Nearest airports: Thiruvananthapuram International Airport and Cochin International Airport, both about 140 kms away.

Chundan Vallam (Snake Boat)

Different classes of native boats participate in the annual boat races of Kerala. The pride of place is occupied by the snake boats or *Chundan Vallams*. Bearing a remarkable resemblance to Polynesian war boats, Kerala's *Chundans* too were adapted in the 16th century by the erstwhile princely states of southern Kerala to meet the requirements of their armies. Today the boats are used only for races. One can see *Chundan Vallams* at Aranmula, Champakkulam or Kuttanadu.

Abhyangasnana

Abhyanga or whole body application of herbal oil was part of Keralites' daily routine and it helped them maintain good health in a tropical environment. Today you can avail of it at accredited ayurvedic spas, hotels and resorts as well as at ayurvedic hospitals. One is supposed to recline in seven different positions, while medicated oil is massaged all over the body in about 45 minutes.

Panchakarma

The word *Panchakarma* literally means 'five actions'. This is a five pronged method of treatment designed for the expulsion of *Amams* (internal toxins that cause diseases) from the human body. *Panchakarma* therapy can be availed under the supervision of a physician at accredited ayurvedic spas in resorts and hotels or at accredited ayurvedic hospitals.

Panchakarma

Houseboats

In the old days the inland waterways were the major channels of transport and country boats were the principal means of transportation. *Kettuvallams* were boats *(vallams)* with built up sides *(Kettu)*. Traditionally they were poled to move. People used these boats for long trips. Today these boats have been modified by adding plush bedrooms, attached bathrooms, modern kitchens, living rooms and breezy balconies. There are several points throughout Kerala from where you can hire houseboats.

Festivals of Kerala

No matter which month one visits Kerala, there is always a festival unfolding in some corner of the state. However, the weeks before and after the main Onam festival (August - September) offer a wide range of related festivals. The busy temple festival season begins in November and lasts till May. For the dates and times of these festivals visit the official website of Kerala Tourism, www.keralatourism.org.

Houseboat

A festival procession

Kathakali

Kathakali

The principal classical dance form of Kerala where the characters use *Mudras* or highly sophisticated hand gesture language along with eloquent facial expressions to convey the story. A spectacular costume, rich and colourful headgear and make-up transform the characters into larger than life visions on stage. Vocal musical rendering occurs only as a backdrop along with percussion and gongs. Each Kathakali artiste is the product of years of dedicated toil often starting from childhood.

Mohiniyattam

Mohiniyattam a classical solo dance form of Kerala, is the dance of the enchantress – a slow and sensuous performance using highly specialised *Mudras* or hand sign language. The costume of ivory handloom clothes with broad gold brocade and traditional Kerala jewellery lends Mohiniyattam a characteristic flavour of the land.

Mohiniyattam

Kutiyattam

Kutiyattam is the ancient form of Sanskrit theatre which has kept alive its vibrant tradition for over 2000 years and has been honoured by UNESCO as 'One of the Masterpieces of Oral and Intangible Heritage of Humanity'. Traditionally, Kutiyattam performances are staged in theatres called *Koothambalams* and accompanied by such instruments as the *Mizhavu, Edakka* and *Kuzhithaalam*.

Theyyam

Theyyam is a temple dance of northern Kerala. Theyyam incorporates dance, mime and music and enshrines the rudiments of ancient shamanistic cultures which attached great importance to the worship of heroes and the spirits of ancestors. There are over 400 Theyyams. Theyyams are usually performed each year from December to April.

Kutiyattam

Theyyam

Chenda

Chenda is an essential accompaniment to Kathakali, the classical dance drama of Kerala. In ancient times, Chenda was drummed for heralding temple festivities, announcements or royal decrees. An integral part of all festivals and processions in Kerala, Chenda's rhythmic beat carries far. Crafted carefully by covering both ends of a hollow wooden cylinder with bull hide drawn tight with cotton ropes, it is played with two slightly curved drumsticks.

The Rendezvous **Book** of **Kerala**

Panchavadyam

Pancha (five) *Vadyam* (instrument) is an orchestra, typical of Kerala, consisting of five instruments – *Maddalam, Edakka, Thimila, Kombu and Ilathalam*. The first three are percussion instruments. *Kombu,* literally meaning horn, is a 'C' shaped wind instrument and *Ilathalam* is a native version of the cymbals.

Koothambalam

Koothambalams are the theatres within the premises of temples, where certain temple art forms are staged. The sage Bharata, who wrote *Natyasastra*, an exhaustive treatise on dramaturgy, prescribed the specifications of the temple theatre. Other *Koothambalams* have been constructed outside temples in recent past, which anyone can visit.

They are:
(1) Vailoppilli Samskrithi Bhavan, Thiruvananthapuram city.
(2) Kerala Kalamandalam, Cheruthuruthy, Thrissur.

Panchavadyam

Koothambalam

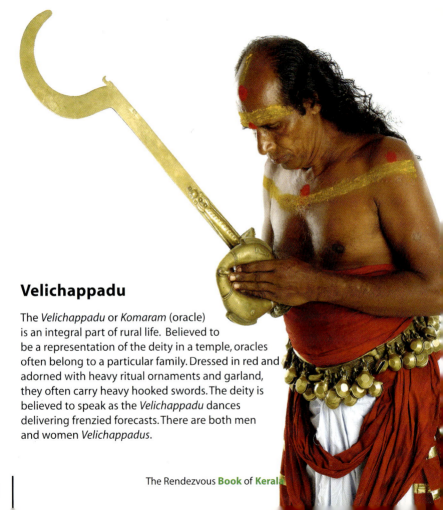

Velichappadu

The *Velichappadu* or *Komaram* (oracle) is an integral part of rural life. Believed to be a representation of the deity in a temple, oracles often belong to a particular family. Dressed in red and adorned with heavy ritual ornaments and garland, they often carry heavy hooked swords. The deity is believed to speak as the *Velichappadu* dances delivering frenzied forecasts. There are both men and women *Velichappadus*.

The Rendezvous **Book** of **Kerala**

Astrology

Regular consultations with astrologers at every important turn of life is quite common in Kerala. Once a baby is born its horoscope is written by an astrologer making calculations based on the date, time and place of birth. A visit to one of these would be intriguing to know your past, present and future.

Nilavilakku

Nilavilakku is a standing oil and wick lamp. Lighting this lamp in the morning and evening is an important ritual of traditional Hindu families and is considered an auspicious act often done on various occasions. Many functions and projects are inaugurated in Kerala with the lighting of a *Nilavilakku*, the local equivalent of ribbon cutting.

River Kabini

One of the best-kept secrets in Wayanad is the wide range of experiences that the river Kabini offers. Tucked deep within the forests of Wayanad, a long stretch of Kabini winds through a cluster of tiny islands called the Kuruwa dweeps. Here you can enjoy nature in its finest splendor as you raft along the gurgling river.

Nearest railway station: Kozhikode, about 138 kms away.
Nearest airport: Karipur Airport, about 113 kms away.

Astrologer

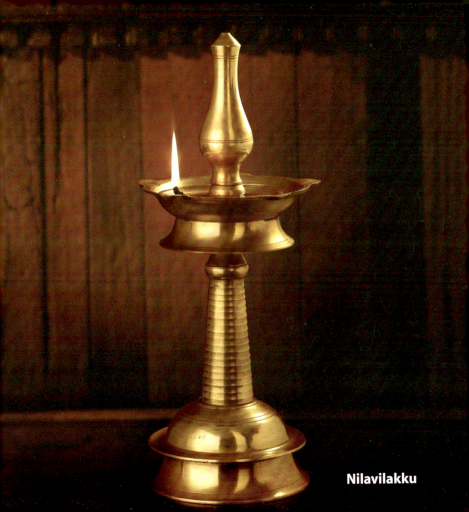

Nilavilakku

Kanikonna

Kanikonna

Kanikonna or Indian Laburnum (*Cassia fistula*) is a tree with golden yellow flowers. This has officially been accepted as the state flower of Kerala. Keralites have an emotional attachment with these flowers as they see them as the symbol of prosperity and abundance. This is a seasonal flower. You can see the trees in bloom in February - April, in time for the *Vishu* festival.

Nalukettu

Built by the wealthier sections of society, *Nalukettu* can be explained as an expansion on the concept of *Sala* enshrined in *Vastusasthra*, the Indian science of architecture. An *Ekasala* is a house with just a square or rectangular room with *Verandahs*. When the four sides are closed by additional Salas, the resultant square house becomes *Chatussala* or the *Nalu* (four) *Kettu* (built up sides) with an open central courtyard.

Elephant wearing Nettippattom

Nettippattom

In Malayalam, *Nettippattom* means an ornament to decorate the forehead. Interestingly, *Nettippattoms* are the ornaments used to decorate the foreheads of elephants. *Nettippattoms* are made of an elongated triangular cloth with apex down, which fits the front of an elephant's head. The cloth with corners rounded is fully decorated with shiny copper bubbles and gold plated crescents.

Coir Products

Coir is rope made from coconut fibres. Coir was traditionally used to bind together and caulk the hull and deck planks of not only local boats but also the famous Arab trading ships like Dhows and *Urus*. Besides the manufacture of ropes of various thicknesses, coir was woven into beautiful floor carpets, doormats and even decorative wall hangings.

Uru

There is a thriving indigenous shipbuilding industry around Beypore, near Kozhikode, an old port of Kerala. The sailing vessels made here are called *Urus* in the local language. For centuries Arab traders have had their ships made here and plied them along their traditional offshore trade route extending from Zanzibar all the way to Canton in China. The wooden vessels are normally 30 metres long, 10 metres wide and some seven metres high.

Gathering of monsoon clouds

Murals

Traditionally rendered in five colours with brushes using dyes made from plant extracts and minerals, these 'semi-fresca' works have wonderfully stood the tests of time. The murals at Padmanabhapuram, Krishnapuram and Mattanchery palaces offer insightful vistas into Kerala's rich cultural heritage. Murals in the Christian tradition can be found in the churches at Kanjoor, Angamali, Cheppadu and Paliekkara.

Sadya - Traditional Kerala Feast

Sadya is usually served as lunch on a broad banana leaf. Just inside the outer rim of the long leaf platter a variety of side dishes are served ranging from a ripe plantain fruit, *papads*, chips and pickles at left through a variety of chutneys and savouries ending in a vegetable curry called *Aviyal* to the right of the guest. The main fare, rice is served in the centre in one or two helpings each eaten with a different curry like *Dal* mixed with ghee or *sambhar*, with frequent forays to the side dishes around the rim. A selection of sweet dishes called *Payasams* follows.

Monsoon

There are two rainy seasons – the main South-west Monsoon coming in June-July and the North-east Monsoon coming in October-November. The heavy showers of the South-west Monsoon hit Thiruvananthapuram in the first week of June and go on to drench the rest of the sub-continent. Together the monsoons decorate Kerala in its mosaic of green and high yellow. Monsoon time is also ideal for the ayurvedic rejuvenation therapy.

Mural painting can be learnt at the regular long-term courses run by the Guruvayoor Devaswom Institute of Mural Painting, East Nada, Guruvayoor or at the Vijnana Kalavedi, Aranmula.

Sadya

Kasavu Mundu

Mundu (dhoti) is a light pure white or cream coloured cotton handloom cloth worn by Keralites. It is an approximately 6 feet x 4 feet rectangle, often in double layer, wound around the waist by both men and women. *Kasavu* is the gold or silver brocade border used to decorate the richer varieties of *Mundu*. Today they are worn only on special occasions. Men wear *Mundu* with a shirt and women wear *Mundu* along with a blouse to cover the upper torso.

Spices of Kerala

The Phoenicians and Egyptians are said to have established trade relations with Kerala as early as 3000 BC. Evidence of this spice trade has been found in Kodungalloor, which the Greeks and Romans knew as the port of Muziris before it silted up and Kochi became the leading port. It is believed that cinnamon from Kerala was used to embalm the bodies of dead Pharaohs in Egypt. In those days Kerala was known as the Malabar coast. The main components of trade were sandalwood and spices – black pepper, cardamom, ginger, clove and cinnamon.

Kurumulaku (Black Pepper)

Black gold or black Pepper (Family name: *Piper nigrum*, Botanical name: Piperaceae), *Kurumulaku* grows in abundance in the fertile soil of Kerala. Seeing this high green vine, which yields the most popular spice in the world, in its natural habitat is a must for any visitor. Kerala's pepper and spices changed world history when Europeans sailed to these coasts in search of them. In Wayanad district of northern Kerala and Idukki district of central Kerala you can see pepper vines in abundance.

Karicku (Tender Coconut)

Karicku in Malayalam means tender coconut.
The sweet juice inside the voluminous tender nutshell is a drink offered even to the gods in the shrines. Ibnu – Batuta (AD 1304 – 1368) the famous African traveller who visited Kerala in 1342 has recorded drinking this delicious nectar of tender coconuts. Apart from the juice, the unhardened white jelly-like nut lining the insides of the shell is also a treat to eat.

Kadumanga

A mouth-watering local mango pickle. Very tender mangoes are picked from the tree and pickled in a special mixture of red chilly and mustard. The mix is aged for six months in a traditional earthenware jar. Kadumanga for the Malayalee is a cultured symbol of the land's culinary essence.

Kappa and Meen Curry (Tapioca and Fish Curry)

Kappa (Tapioca or Cassava) was brought to Kerala from Brazil by a former king of Travancore and it caught on as a favourite supplement to rice. Fish, being abundantly available almost throughout the year, sea, river, and lake fish preparations became the natural choice as side-dishes among the fish-loving populace. The blazing red fish curry, which amply spices up the mild-tasting Kappa to suit native tastes, is the all-time favourite accompaniment. Vegetarians too have a choice of chutneys to go with *Kappa*.

Ada Pradhaman

A sweet dish of Kerala, served as the main desert in the traditional Kerala *Sadya* or feast. Thin sun dried rice flour flakes called *Adas*, made from a special kind of rice, are first steamed. They are then boiled in melted molasses lumps. Thick coconut milk is another major ingredient making the whole into a porridge. Cashew nuts and raisins fried in ghee and ginger and cardamom are added as seasoning. Ready to make instant *Ada Pradhaman* mix packs are now available in most major shops.

Parippuvada

Parippuvada is the most popular snack of Kerala. Any self-respecting eatery in the state is bound to have the crunchy *Parippuvada* to go with cups of piping hot tea or coffee and plantain fruits that are consumed at all times of the day. The *Parippuvada* is circular in shape and made by deep-frying patties of ground *dal* and condiments in coconut oil. Traditionally, Thuvar *dal* is used.

Kanji (Rice gruel)

Kanji is rice cooked in plenty of water, roughly five to six parts of water to one part rice. For a very long time, Kanji was the Keralite's main dish at every meal, seven days a week. In the last fifty years other dishes, mostly rice-based, ousted Kanji from the breakfast table. Salted Kanji is served with accompaniments like ghee, a dry fish chutney, fried *Pappads*, sautéed vegetables and rice crispies, fresh or toasted coconut chutney, *Puzhukku* (vegetables cooked with fresh coconut and cumin) or boiled red beans.

Chips

The speciality of Kerala is banana chips.
Raw bananas (fruit of *Musa paradisiaca*) sliced
into thin discs are deep fried in coconut oil with a pinch of
yellow turmeric powder and salt to taste. You can see roadside
vendors frying these chips in their makeshift mobile stands.
A packet or two of these will keep you good company as you leave
this land of Gods.